Bijou Le Tord

The Little Shepherd

The 23rd Psalm

Delacorte Press   New York

To my brother Yvon,
with love

Published by Delacorte Press
Bantam Doubleday Dell Publishing Group, Inc.
666 Fifth Avenue   New York, New York 10103
Text and illustrations copyright © 1991 by Bijou Le Tord

Library of Congress Cataloging in Publication Data
Le Tord, Bijou
The little shepherd : 23rd Psalm / Bijou Le Tord.
p.   cm.
Summary: Paraphrases in simple language the well-known psalm in
which God is compard to a shepherd.
ISBN 0-385-30417-X. — ISBN 0-385-30418-8 (lib. bdg.)
1. Bible. O.T. Psalms XXIII—Paraphrases, English.   [1. Bible.
O.T. Psalms XXIII—Paraphrases.]   I. Title.
BS1450 23rd.L38   1991
223'.205209—dc20   90-49039   CIP   AC

Manufactured in the United States of America

October 1991

10   9   8   7   6   5   4   3   2   1

The text of this book is set in sixteen-point ITC Zapf International, a typeface designed
by Hermann Zapf in 1977. The illustrations are done in Windsor Newton watercolors
on Arches 140-pound cold-press watercolor paper.
Typography by Lynn Braswell.

Psalm 23

A PSALM OF DAVID

The Lord is my shepherd; I shall not want.

2 · He maketh me to lie down in green pastures: he leadeth me beside the still waters.

3 · He restoreth my soul: he leadeth me in the paths of righteousness for his name's sake.

4 · Yea, though I walk through the valley of the shadow of death, I will fear no evil: for thou art with me; thy rod and thy staff they comfort me.

5 · Thou preparest a table before me in the presence of mine enemies: thou anointest my head with oil; my cup runneth over.

6 · Surely goodness and mercy shall follow me all the days of my life: and I will dwell in the house of the Lord forever.

FROM THE *King James Version*
[1611]

The Lord

is my shepherd

I will not
need much

to make me happy
each day

I sit with Him
in a field

and I am peaceful

He shows me

where water
runs,
quietly

His Love
gives
me strength

and when
He guides me
and shows me

the path of goodness

I know He is
my shepherd

even if I walk

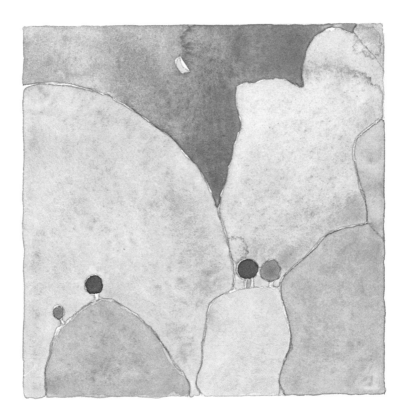

in the night

I will not
be afraid
or be hurt

because, Lord,
You are with me
and I feel
reassured

You give
me
food

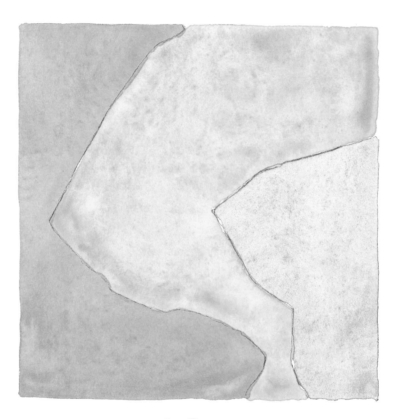

in front

of my enemies

and
pour
sweet
and scented
oil upon my head

my cup is full

in
the morning
and in the
night
His Love will
follow me

and
I will live
in the house
of the Lord

for a long,
long time.